Famous Hermits

Stacy Szymaszek

Praise for *Famous Hermits*

"We have no choice but to love our lyricism hungry, insistent and outgoing in withdrawal. It has to sound like something as it rounds the corner, down the steps and through the park into a broken city left behind for chaparral. *Famous Hermits* is a book about how we share necessity through sequestration, moving for love, if we can. Made by a poet who loves poetry, it makes a beautiful argument for poetry. Szymaszekal music won't stop midstride, midlife, midline, and we have to love that."

— Fred Moten

"The poems in *Famous Hermits* take surface narrative and give it deep glide, that deeper dive that happens when you approach the world as your confidante. Within a few lines, Szymaszek interlaces eons worth of intricate history to galvanize a poet's hangout. She shows her mastery of line and form by encapsulating cinematic propulsions that glint, in a flash, to then come back to our daily dialogue. Infiltrating cohesion with density, and a razor sharp wit, the poet's "elite city" appears as a temporal embrace in the heat of a desert, an embodiment of our migratory needs. This richly focused collection explores our diurnal awakenings as cognitive planes, where each grouping of text is a radial entity, a hermetic investigation of a poet's walk."

— Edwin Torres

"Sometimes all it takes is becoming a hermit. Continuing her exploration of the poem-as-diary with this new ecstatic collection, Stacy Szymaszek proves herself a glorious master of the aphorism, the bon mot, and the scintillating image. Somewhere between memory and shouting for joy are these lines."

— Lucy Ives

Published in the United States by:
Archway Editions,
a division of powerHouse Cultural Entertainment, Inc.
32 Adams Street, Brooklyn, NY 11201

www.archwayeditions.us

Daniel Power, CEO
Chris Molnar, Editorial Director
Nicodemus Nicoludis, Managing Editor
Naomi Falk, Editor

Library of Congress Control Number: 2022935999

ISBN 978-1-57687-980-1

Printed by Toppan Leefung

First edition, 2022

10 9 8 7 6 5 4 3 2 1

Interior layout by Nicodemus Nicoludis
Cover art: KB Jones

Printed and bound in China

ARCHWAY
EDITIONS

Famous Hermits

Stacy Szymaszek

Archway Editions, Brooklyn, NY

CONTENTS

FUN METER

1.

Mark   today I learn his name
          is Mark   fastened to his apron
a button that says
          FUN METER   arrow turned to "high"   I like your fun
meter   *it goes up a little   each time someone says*
          that   he suggests sipping this stout room
temp with my feet up by the fire   this market is a mountain
outpost   an aisle of hot sauce   and greeting cards   ah clear vision
                    Mark   here I am   my left foot   by the blue
reconcile   my life spent guarding   against   surprise
attack   leave the gun / take the cannoli   I ratted on
          my family   a gay falcon   C. reading Duncan
saying I AM DUNCAN   and that is my sad knowing   who among
          us belongs   to a failed
mission   do not read on   read Parra   a dose of ANTI
Dunparra!
in the blood boil of high romance   where H.D. is a little bony
          but   *all to the mustard*   lads   they shred his flawed logic   I say
it's like going to a holy place and seeing a reliquary of crutches
          cheers to the poet who told me never to read another Whitman poem
"read Auden" but it turns out that old crab has more tenderness
in one wrinkle

W. wonders if the classroom is an extension of the state
come to room 210
research every name that comes out of my mouth

2.

if you
are still
reading this
the truth is
my lover
turned my
glasses into
dust drank
cords of me and
built our house
broke the bed fucking
I'm going to show you
upper limit fucking
what I learned when next we
swank for fucking
which will be
I assume
before dawn

die fucking
die fucking
can't tonight

rooster goat   cat bunny bunny cat

whippet at the crook   rooster train whistle

finding her by decibel   desert red bat

3.

I prime a crew
once upon a page
words are sacred
don't edit
scrapit   another one primes a crew
                                   devotes herself to rightly
                                   place their every word

CHRIST

4.

somewhere in Brooklyn there is
                a storage space   of all of my likes and dislikes
and the uncertainty of "the Boss" cock
                             in a blue suitcase with a painting
                 I should like better

today I could not remember
myself in the early aughts
        check her records
                upon a golden cushion
                of a Danish modern chair

I am often invited to hear told   the decline
                of the grandmothers   my prophets of conflict
                one of them hides her own teeth
                        though in a moment of lucidity tries to teach
                                Sheepshead to someone in a fugue state

alert of government issued weather report
                from the financial capital   my closest bank
branch is in Idaho   last week when I couldn't
        sleep   I tried to predict the market   cardinal
                with a fat check   we ate eggs in Tucson

and later that night she put a litany
        in my ear   lit row after row of tapers
                my fist was a bell   and her back a tower   I bawled
                Spira, spera   mingled
                into one angel

                green leaves over
                a heart in ruins

                GOTH
                HUGO   it is
                true   …   my crow Pluto

a psychic home
for our coffee   has clear glass windows

5.

P. dreams Ozzy Osborne is
my real father   *I love you all; I love you more than life itself*
                                but you're all fucking mad!

A. says *tell her I say thank you*
        for rescuing Stacy   A. has sat with all of our corpses
and said Buddhist things   buckle   let go

6.

      stirred for birds
        +
      love
           prove
                    move   +   buckle
                                      high there
                                      no wonder of it

the priest has a watch
tells the 12 stations of the cross
Bishop lost her mother's watch
the priestess has no watch
E. recites Prufrock in a trance with she/her pronouns

        the Ladies of Night Prosody laugh

Cocteau Twins first US TV appearance
Liz took great liberties with her voice on "Bluebeard"
making it even more inaccessible
        and wore a monastic garment!

            + we have always known you wanted us

7.

each of my steps   boot chains to ice   echoic foot
        the walk home from prosody   we can all agree on ode
to even silly things we love

            but can we make amends in dreams?

a tall glass of wool in a western town

                eastward loved imperfectly

    mountain
    ain't got no

    rhymes for me
    give me your morning hand   for hand
           word   for word
                  wet for life
                        tender band
                Baroque

Buddhist

noisy nothing

        capitulate!   at last   no more   to do

airy
devilship
removed

8.

pulled a long shot
like an Americano
    Prince Bestie and I
    relieved to exchange
    a platitude over the phone   me and my Bialetti   snowing sideways
        never walk and drink the dirt   at the same time
I'm fine
        mother is still   my mother   description of a gruesome
murder of a half-Italian   as I steeped with my lover's soap
 ask *who gave me the note?*   they don't wonder
    whose heart was lost   for me to take heart
        everyone who decided against their heart

You will often tell the story. If you do that you/will be able to marry those you love…

    you are going to have so much fun… YES it goes up a little
each time you say…   in NYC the tundra the desert …   we perceive a form
a householder
    of actual meaning   no they don't wonder who fastened it there
        at the same time

in the inference of their care
a sweet burn

we learn slowly   (gnostic)
less stoic bed rolls
record a word   for a word   a regional Baltimore
clean ears for Alidio
stirred in the lower belly

I rest my butch head

CENTURION FACE

1.

New York was hell on earth today
        trash fire on the F track   a black substance   perhaps
mastic asphalt oozing from vents along the C/E
                    but I'm only reading about it   I slipped
on the ice   down to one knee   they don't believe in salt
or plows   and I forgot the chains for my feet   "At Night the States"
        closes with Montana   a word I have always liked   the state
grows on me   like adulthood   still I confess I ate hot
                        cereal out of a pot   at midnight   and it tasted
like and was the same color as the rug in here   so when a glob
fell I left it there   so I wouldn't lose my thought   it was Marlowe's
birthday   yesterday and I heard the ground hog
insinuated   early spring   my love cares to list the pleasures
        of going down on me   like a vine
I spiral all over the house
                        I looked up the Duncan line
in "The Torso" and it was Marlowe and it was his birthday
        maybe we are babies   with fire eyes   forever
                    what could be done   for friends not to grow
                                apart?
and how is it
that we are with each other everywhere?   and why does the quiver

of kyanite   never stab this marshmallow heart
journeyer toast   an ethos   fuss above the heat –
      she says of her hand   her home is inside me   unlocking
chambers of my female body   then live with me
                  come next arctic grip   snow carried by wind into drifts
is called driven   pull sleeping gown of roughest wool
across yielding skin   centurion face   four-wheel drive
      I writhe   I am a human I think

2.

I am I because my landlord is my accountant   he knows me
      in the tyranny of paperwork gesticulate over a plank
of leather   with our drugstore readers   the ones I launched across
a café yesterday while making a lesser point   Montana is sitting
on enough coal to power the country
      for 100 years—alas
      he staples NY under MT   calls me a resident   by day
I melted an icicle in my mouth   by night my love asked me what can I do
now because of what   I've done   the archive is tousled
      evidence of the org in my hands—ok
                              look
                              back   frag- fig-

                              o a fir

                              quickens
                              brushes window
                                    it's 1 degree

I like the way he breezes
                through paper

one more poem *if you think you can*
handle it   starting with the same line
makes it possible to write more
than a refrain

                                        one thinks it's the last
                                        elegy then
                                        sludge pouring
                                        civic veins

it burns like a red hot coal for the ancient heavenly connection in New York's snow

GRANZINO THE SECOND

the only sounds I heard last night were my boot steps
       boiling water   and the ringing in my ears that started
in 2002   I no longer reside within
      a church   or within earshot of bells   lost friend
      touched my face in a dream   and I told her how lonely
I had been using ESP   today I woke up to loping wind   welcomed
another sound   in the quietest mountain village
      never any reason to force anything   boots laced   water
boiling   my sociality   stored banter
                             B: Am I being clear?
                             A: (from audience) Ya.

some knew this might be useful
      to other people   *you have mastered*
                       butch winter   I wear animals
             and gain new knowledge of my own body
          as in   what becomes of it
once glided down her
throat   *you are beautiful I want to take off your underwear*

          a crasser order undoes my shame   so I am her King
with a twist   a fir   coronet   lick her mid hriff
tame a faun   Granzino
the Second
        end stop biological fathers on westward trains

"but you shall not escape my iambics"   the news is   we are prone
to the prosody of torpor   heartbeats they will never discover

all the liquids I poured were nearly black   fernet   coffee   stout
          either I am rock or tree   to quietly free my poor history

an eggshell in Polish amber

BLOOD OF A POET

1.

I breathe in the downstairs couple's routine meals
        today some kind of stew   do I live on Pluto
or another celestial snowball?

        draining bath water sounds like a minimalist score
                        with peopled melody   my artifacts are enough
in order   we don't want more exes   especially if a lesbian
        mode might not be known in 20 years

ME TANGERE   call me anti-Christ   the bond must
        be physical   the tomb peopled   observe my artifacts
            an ant farm with a queen   but haven't we always
                                                             been besieged?

        jeered dream of a nonviolent mafia

                                                             kill them
                                                             with
                                                                 kind-
                                                                 ness

2.

heard my name on Ludlow   oh God   there's another one

I know the names…
I know. But I do not have the proof. I don't even have clues.

retraced steps on the grid
        in the change city
                split bowl of Italian chicory   her hand squeezed my
                                                side keeping pace with
                                              a monk's heart
        I'm an adorable reindeer
        Why don't I fit in?

                        structures set up to be weird   heaven
                                                    earth

as if I showed up to my memorial in a
a colorful jacket   greeted   by   a controversy
                                        of poets

3.

        author   augment
                        authentic   those with police powers

procedural   lovers
                        bewitched in spaces   of yielded sway

the world is of infinitely great roughness

the music is not what it is said to be   held

hell   tonic sound

CHOCOLATE SARDINES

outside the ice cream shop

we speak silent
     solve silent
         then herein

4.

mid-age morning
vulnerability   wakened fists at chest
bald and breathing like a baby   again doing something in dreams
that I cannot do

        what is it in me   that does that?

hopping down a city block on one foot past the guards
as the city and my foot grows with my hate and love

why did I turn the east side of my Great Lakes city into New York City
replete with bells of St. John's and the garrets of elder visionaries left to us

lost friend started to make a casserole but I couldn't stay and i couldn't tell
her   took her spool of ribbon to Lake Park giving her the chance

to become a no-show

whatever can come to a woman can come to me

5.

a good café will not have
robots doing pour-overs   we come up against the academy
                              and make panic work for us   I want men
like Elaine De Kooning   painted them   doing nothing
and not solemn about it   even JFK
      and poets that wipe their faces with time
what you think is what you do   the long take   I entered the archive
and got a sick stomach
too much coffee
plus inexorable rings   too many barrels of ink
                        too many separate accounts of our making

6.

not since puberty had I been so
antagonized   she peaked to   the very next week
decline   except for the ability to amply tell of it
to those who will bear the sight
of me
          A WALKING GROVE OF TREES
                              faculty meetings

Vatican-mind
hide the villains
from the victims   I have pension-envy   keep it paranoid

                    facere   *facilis*

the delusional will only come away with 10% of your meaning

                         late nights via crackling line
                         we portray each other in a way
                         that makes us feel human again

like De Kooning i am devoted to portraits
the thousands of sketches I make of you to know how you are
if you are
            human

HOW RUCKUS IS TEA

                    the pilot announced "the weather in Missoula
        is nice"
                        vague omen

here
   the plant is 3 inches   to the left   and a bottle of bourbon appeared
           on my university desk   which a student told me is not mine
it's the poet's before me   who wanders the town
beside herself   while I marvel in her multiple editions of marvell

                                    the weather is nicety

        I repeatedly step on an envelope
                    from TIAA slipped under my door by the landlord couple

the onion peeled to putrescence
        a solid house for heterosexual sex on mute

no mail allowed here   and if we see you smoking anywhere near here we'll
keep your money and repaint the walls here

        I am soothed by the light   don't trust their proffered
                                                          connection to the land

upon which my movements invent funny grace
between precarity
and   autonomy   corporeal aging head down   cultivates
                                                        sensate bruiser

                    big poetry money to secret fascist
                    branches   drunk
                    on... birdsong
                    old as... creosote!

deep cleaning crew
TOO CLOSE 4 COMFORT
you can bleach away my juice
but you can't un-hear the gasps of my lover

                I don't mind the rain on my head   (no to surplus
        umbrella offer)   as much as I mind the Wild West No Chain

                                        of Command   as another man-

                baby

pukes in the punch bowl

                if I could i would   make their grandchild

                    LIKE ME

    we laugh loud
                    tip toe through the ding-dongs
                                        how ruckus is tea

I'm "worth a million"
       and paid 96% less
sure leave the grapes on my desk

                   my colleague's olden sock
                   monkey heard everything

                       — for P & K

WHAT I ATTACH TO ARE HER DECIMALS

coffee aroma fueled insomniac
dreams   all ambition to vacate the premises in 7 days
                                                in 1 piece

        Tucson calling   it's all very old-fashioned

both Western   and Medieval   I am skirting the robes
        tho cannot   evade what my idolatry beckons

 so I roster   a chair
    my weight made kindling   a goblet that crashed off the sill
                                as I aired out   perhaps made
                                            in Art

                                        and blood
                                            on the microfiber
watched 2 documentaries on Kevyn Aucoin
and cried too much   sounding some doomy pop theory about the cups
of queers raised in the '80s never
having a bottom   FALSE BOTTOMS?!   pour anything into us… do we
                                only become more self-contained?

Also   Aucoin   give us back our eyebrows

                I am I because my eyebrows are knowing wolves
                slabs of knowing

                                        (you jerk)
I am a beautiful butch with
high cheek bones I was born to be good
at knowing
what I hate

                        ergo capitalism

as if dividing my things into further storage units
can obscure my consumer history   books and beds and bikes
                                              my body takes me on a ride
                        I effloresce

maintaining some cardinal grip
on concepts of why funders fund   #1-3   boil source into ethos

6 figures your salvation –
       no   the toilet you went down to find it
                   overflows

there are many who make
                              their dissent palatable   and they will keep
                                                    bearing children
white tail specks on the mountain
red tail speck in the sky   from a tub I won't see the likes of
                            my sottoprogramma   of laxity
let us to our royalties
                         my home on the edge of another campus
     where my love notes   passersby taking pictures of the purple cactus
and reports that a larger Bialetti makes her
                   wonder if she has shrunk
what I attach to

are her decimals

                                  the infinity of ways to kiss any inch of her

and knowing

               any inch of me is knowable to her

THIS IS THE FIRST DAY OF OUR LIVES!

I took the self-portrait actively thinking this
      reawakened thought   in addition to the usual

                HERE IS A LIVING DYKE

no poet or theorist has ever helped me
      understand "queering time"   'tis all the rage

            as much as aging

noon bells toll from a modest Lutheran church to the north
      I don't know the hymn

    a fraternity to the west   and east a plot teeming with cacti

in a way people weren't meant to live here   city in a desert   people
collapse in the middle of crosswalks and then   people
     come out of nowhere to help
              Crabbd ambiguity
              of lost connections
    never have I been so close to

                  Bisbee

airing gnarly

     the put-on words of quasi-populists   buggin' me

my lover assuages me   a box of pink peonies
                     I deem cute
                                the one that is still a knob

says there is   space created for us
                                   when the deceived look at them

           perhaps I was to blame in my adherence
              to the image of me as altruistic

      prognostic tumbleweeds   at least leave seeds in
                         alleys of friendship

what may be a heat rash may be addressed
by switching to boxers
                          put yourself and your cotton
                          through the ringer

                    YOU SIR ARE A YET LIVING DYKE

every symptom is a symptom of
the maelstrom of hellish but completely necessary change
        pulling snapdragons from my cunt

            silence
                 everyone   I'm tending to my hygiene

listening to the doves who love water yet densely populate
              Sonoran mornings

     Esperanza cuts my hair every 2 weeks and reflects my vitality *it grows so fast*   silence

so gracious
and mutual

we have been badly taught
"sticks and stones will break my bones but…"

in these massive shapes I only hope to make supple
my complexities

WISDOM OF THE DESERT

I was a sucker for Saint Oil in a triangular apothecary
jar   even blue   applied it to venous blood upon the wrists

        as close as I came to being an insane cleric
who believes ordination brings ontological change   poets
                and priests
                   who believe
      they are beings of a different order   bring trouble

statues of Saint Catherine abound   of course   the Catalinas
      but so named by Kino   (an Italian)   after his
         sister's favorite saint   who became more beautiful the more she was
             scourged

              BABAD DO'AG
                  the range already had a name
try to vary the maxims
a stone in the mouth   like a yoga prop   to practice when to compel the flesh
to speak
        patience as I am not   full tenor   belting pristine messages
                 to those who want me
take me to Phoenix for my 50th
      where I can rise from exploit
                know that vigilance is a blanket

                              left in a grotto   deter neck spurs

              a fleet of night bicyclists appeared as red flashes on the grounds below

a therapist mistook my hair for a dormant militant streak   ok with the reminder

                                                        practice gets me closer

        who called me lady
who worried about my body been large
        who asked me not to wear a chain wallet
who searched my drop crotch
        who said cover your ink
who pawned me to cover
                                        true   tough
                                                love

                                        I can breathe out your malice
                                                        in private

        who were the female teachers
"who knew everything"
        (Duncan   Olson   Rexroth)
who were described as polymaths
        whose wayward tomes are reprinted

oh Hypatia
torn apart   in Alexandria by a Christian mob with clam shells
                        whereas Catherine (of Alexandria)
                                was scourged by pagans for converting other pagans
                                        to Christians
        domain of bobcats

sharp-crested

life as you knew it   a city fully encroached

vegetables rotting
in neighbor's minds   tonight word games   *motors lotions*
against dementia +

storing clothes in a trunk for
her future use

STOP MAKING PEACE

an orange collapsed and rotted in the dirt
      parking lot
            I have steered evil clear   thus far

a double fisted baby   who knows a devil's turds   the feudal
      property lady   can't let go of me insinuating I disappeared

"a photograph of tree bark"   perhaps standing in for distress that I
moved   into the hutch
        the ashes of two Golden Retrievers
           and left my DNA on the rugs

           I talk to the lizards doing push-ups
in the trees   last night's dream a circus of bugs   a roach so mighty
it dragged one of my shirts across the room   distant freight horns sent me
     into a doze and doves
         in the citrus woke me
                  I'd lob the orange
                  befitting the jester-image state-crafted for us
        alas it would turn into a mythological ball of sun
            and my dreadful martyrdom has run its course
in the book mart
     we compare translations of the first canto of HELL
        go with Dorothy Sayers 1949   crime writer and poet
    speaks in the intro of how we have recently rediscovered the problem

                                                    of power
          there is no allegorical masque   were we all trying
to look bigger in the '80s in imposing oversized suits?
          telling people it's a double Windsor when it's a simple knot
               because the photographs uphold that
                                        you are a giant

     the hard admission   when we give a hand job   to power
          we are corollary   and bootless poems never get
                                             written
                    Enter freely, Go safely,
               And leave something of the happiness you bring.

                                   I know the names…
     the dentist asked me if I was in pain
                    my teeth lined up to break out of mortal coil
                    I love a tough babe   the second old man to high-
          five me in two days   the other being a handyman   after I helped him
install the air   all of the dentist's crowns were gold
                                        like those of ancient Luzon
I have lounged with lions
               some Gotham enemies
some on pedestals at San Xavier   with my wax hat protecting my face
          where all four deserts in the US converge   and four
               mountain ranges   my cry

                    in the sloppy middle of life

          is a dialogue   in view of Santa Catalina

               I woke to find

40

an elder woman selling her soap

    mine has more

        pine tar

  in it

        because frankly

  I am

    a master

        of my trade

ANTIPOETRY

the whole thing began with a
NIGHT MARCH OF ENERGUMENS
through the center of the city

the dachshund I was walking turned into an iguana

I tore through piles of wool

then in a fast food break room my temper startled two friends

how many times do I have to quit this job?

it's a marathon march through the harshest elements on earth   :::   monsoons
haboobs
a boiling sun

the energumens spied on us at the aviary/buffet   laureates
among them

THE FIELDS OF SOUND
LEARNING DEVASTED   scrapbooks passed off in succulents

       my dress   a janky silk shirt and drawstring
           pants

            my brimmed hat smelled of grandfather wired

the same   to make a penny per button

            are you shocked to discover someone in the arts

has a blue-collar job?
                      celebrity
                      city   afford me anon-
                      ymity

      observed us from armored car   to figure out robot simulacrum

           with skeletal hand emerging from the abdomen

that senses cash and rakes it in   [their gaze was calm during rush hour
                      draining words dry as the river's bed]

              but our prosody is sound   in time +
              our history the practice of space   in time
                                THEN

              I was satisfied

that I had seen   and been

seen

ENOUGH

Petrarch to Boccaccio :::

such is the period

in which we live

and are growing old

FAMOUS HERMITS

"I saw myself
a ring of bone
in the clear stream
of all of it"

  –   Lew Welch
          from "The Hermit Songs"

"I know that you've been conditioned to… become famous, and make your mark,
and all that kind of thing, but you won't go very far…".

  –   Agnes Martin
          *Transcribed from her talk "Going Up in the Tower" at The Poetry Project, March 6,
          1980*

///

we tell ourselves stories to darken our moods
     before they do   delving into historical imagination
we turn up a deficit in the language of men
     young ones can
and do kill for him
     infiltrating mock empathy   deploying words
such as "terrible"   while rubbing his hands together
     an occultist running a country
perhaps we need to permit ourselves propaganda
     to use sound
arch
sly   oft'
ugly   and check records for those who fought
     fire with poetry
sometimes a prophecy is simply everyone
     admitting everything we know
at the same time
ergo truth
     the privilege of knowing your craft is
it is yours to abandon   the low spirit arrives   we call ourselves the same word
     but are animated by different concerns   creating another they

///

I'm not generating a personality in a non-industrialized city
setting inquisitive energy free

how childlike both my attachment and outrage
        that they are avidly hunted   who would fucking kill
a dove –
duh
        who wouldn't?   this morning
I watched the agent walk a repairman around the house
        remembered when my mother was an agent and I drew
a mustache on her portrait
        when it rains the room where I write poems
leaks from two different microcracks   why I think this is
        vital information has to do with unburying oneself
from a heap of devices   a literary system
        I can't live in

      ///

    what is it to leave an elite
city of the world
    where people go to succeed
it's threatening when people leave "the best community available"
    because it may be that we have given up on the dream
you can get sober in a bar!
    sociologists say social people live longer
but I wonder if this is true for women for whom camaraderie feels lethal
    after a career in hyper-accommodation
or any woman making work of her inwardness   an art hermit

or my 100-year old grandmother vitalized by her relationship
with her Lord   listening to news of the mad world unfold
        as she said it would
I finally agreed to get on the scale
        my new doctor didn't say anything about my weight
which has returned since leaving the elite city
        rolling in a chair through
six months in ice
        six months in sun scorch
I may have held the only feasible job for my personality
        and you know what they say about lesbians
and women
and butches
and fat
and women
over 50
childless
single
or divorced

                                ///

                new emotional temples alter the universal
                        emit new messages   she is out of her sphere of
                influence   the universe doesn't know what to dish me
                        for work   did service jobs longer than I ran an org
                I reenter 29 and see what I would have done differently
                        and still I end up blocks away from a writing program
                with tenured prose writers teaching poetry because there is no money

///

       braless concealed in an oversized white cotton tee
what may be a hot flash at a gallery
       or feelings about seeing the portrait of a young Black poet I know
put in context with white corporate republican poets
(chancellors   laureates)
       the photographer who traces his lineage back to Whitman
devised concepts for the poets to enact
       based on his reading of their poems
he favors the fantastical
       over the daily

it's a risk to stare into the authoritarian abyss
       their cash demands unquestioned collaboration
with their death drive
       you think you won't but you will
have to abuse your imagination
       obscure your details
to relate to them
       adopt cynicism
think everyone wants what they gave you

///

       ĕrēmīta is the Latinization of the Greek ἐρημίτης
             (erēmitēs) "of the desert" which comes from ἔρημος (erēmos)
       signifying
             desert

uninhabited
hence desert-dweller
in the 13th c. the church's pressure to regularize hermits force
many   women especially   to join established orders
one should never live without accusers to fear
alone in cemeteries
at city gates
on or under bridges
roadsides
mountains
forests
river islands
and the desert
where it was prudent for lone women to dress
in male attire to not be mistaken for a demon
and thrashed

///

I know I'm still unwell because my mind mistakes the shine of a book
for my phone detonating with messages
in case water has memory I stood barefoot in a puddle
a dirt and gravel pothole in our parking lot   and buried my toes
entering the beginning   of a code   inhaling the perfume of a bush
that lives 11,000 years   has been a practice available to me daily
the word "experience" has its roots in "to suffer"   my primary concern is not
for you to relate to me but to honor me as a true other who is nonetheless
a real person
a real poetry

///

a spider living on the cords in a corner of fans
        was here when I returned from New York and the fly was not
in my grass bottomed house shoes I fantasize
        that I live to be wizened and some kid with a good question
finds me   my blazers will have been spread across the country
        pockets unchecked for receipts and lists
moving to the elite city is a ritual as is leaving it
        a certain gesture of hiking your work to a new terrain
if you can imagine poems as having enormous frames

///

it's said that Mary Chapin Carpenter's cover of Lucinda Williams'
"Passionate Kisses" adheres in tempo etc… however
        in the refrain "shouldn't I have this?" Lucinda liquifies the word
"have" perhaps transforming the question into an assumption

am I going overboard?

///

15 Aug. 2019: A YEAR AGO I LEFT THE CITY

spent the morning watching a lizard

on a tree branch they favor   if you say you'll never
do a thing again you deny you are lizard

are any of my five watches still ticking in the locker?
no sooner did I have the thought to buy another
then my phone was showing me Swatch ads
last year in the office I had at least

uttered "Swedish Fish"

before they swam into my feed

///

when the celebration of a laureate is ahistorical
when memory is replaced by ceremony
when we forget other knowledges because we are hit over the head
(when we are One)
when we start a war to get out of depression
when we start a program to give artists status
when we say the opposite of what we mean

"lately when we fuck I feel like we aren't here"
here being America

///

I responded well to the a/c repairman telling me that I looked
　　　　　like "an intelligent woman"　　I knew that the drainage
tube installed at an upward angle was the problem
　　　　　the question that has always gotten me into hot water
BUT WHY?　　(would you do that?)
　　　　　he said people don't take pride in their work and
I flashback – there she is on a tractor running over flowers!
　　　　　what I experienced yesterday　　*I survived another day*
makes me old　　yesterday I was a child

///

worms seen after rain become elegant crane flies
　　　　　I escort one out of the house with a tissue
my Gila monster tee-shirt says I AM NOT A MONSTER
　　　　　but I have overshared　　the Gila likes to come out
after rain to soak in puddles　　iguana handlers say that iguanas
　　　　　seem to prefer certain people over others
which may be an emotion

///

　　　　　a city where people repurpose any item that tethers them
　　　to the past by leaving it on the street　　a city where people delight in

euphoric recall   nostalgia seems so innocent
I dislike when people think everything is fine   not even a nature cure
        cures   or a "health house" or Hockney wearing California tees in
London as he paints through the heartbreak of losing someone indifferent
        to him   I traded sense of outward purpose for autonomy
the tenderest mother can wreck you   just as inviting poets onboard
        very quickly pushes everything to all logical conclusions
only possibly to be born again   somehow doves have air sacs in their
        hollow bones   a woman adapts to her hot hermitage
by the time it is this hot elsewhere you can use what she learned
        debunk a notion of loyalty deeply programmed
in my matrilineage   no one has any claim to me especially those
        who heard my confessions in a smoldering car
our young crypto-fascist moneybags looking ahead circa mid-80s said
        "there might not be a country"
that is nostalgia
that is death drive

        ///

the discourse is crappy   is it a Southwest thing?
        do they think I don't notice that my questions
are being dodged?

                did you ever dare to break it down? (dollars per hour)

        is that a New York thing?   my relentless wonder   the jaw drop
at what must be a dime an hour

or two exams in a row without the doctor touching me   the future of Western
medicine   lab tests and check lists   an American thing?

WE LUMBER INTO POST-REPRODUCTIVE WAITING TO RECEIVE OUR DYKE ILLNESSES

where I tell stories about my body so well   with thoughtful questions
          that aren't explained by repeating the textbook definition of menopause
so well she acts like she's watching Masterpiece Theater

          "you're funny"

                                                                    ///

                              you think you can understand us through your logic
                                        evangelical money cult
                              you think the world wants to be like America
                                        you are a poet but you operate exactly like
                              A POLITICIAN
                                        I am defined by what I am not doing
                              who I used to be
                                        leaning into open questions
                              to slow the inevitable arrival of new identities
                                        do you care about the poem or the poet
                              would you craft poems out of nothing
                                        or   elide with your patron
                              making your life consumable
                                        will our relationship bend
                              or will it
                              break

///

R. wrote "don't be sad"   she is staying near Jean
Seberg's grave and will visit for me   nothing makes me more sad
        than women who don't recover from being destroyed
by an institution   they become lesbians   in dying
        alone   Joan of Arc and Jean   lesbian   the moment of their blanketed
deaths

PERSON A IS CONDEMNED TO DISCREDIT A WHOLE WORLD VIEW WHERE
REALPERSON A LOVES A REALPERSON

who gets credit and discredited   what is life without a public   who remembers what you did
        the rules of heresy simply update like fashion   each decade of rosary
the other night the spirit of art was everywhere as usual   I told Rilke
        that I had examined myself plenty even at a tender age   and there was no power
external and uncorrupt that could judge me   and then I told Sharon
        Olds that her fantasy about going back to tell her parents "don't do it" but knowing
that she wants to live   so "do it" and she bangs them together
        is similarly distressing in that
                                of all things

I go to poetry to free myself from moral imperative

HERE LIES A POET WHO GIVES UP
A CERTAIN MANNER
OF CONTROL

Listen…

(no thanks)

///

The rocks at the wellness center were in small pots
        with descriptions of their powers noted on brown paper   I held rhodonite
with sorrow for all the times I was
(taken for) a ride
(variation of) a man
safe harbor
        but it was moonstone that held me in snowy dreamland with no gravity
something about a poet in concealed backland of a familiar place
        where I would still need sculpturesque boots
in lieu of these grass-bottomed house shoes
        perhaps the question is gaining in the collective   what Duncan meant
by "before the war"   no poet can stand apart or above   all-time
        war   which includes internal
warfare

YOUNG WOMAN: IS OUR ERA WORSE?
HUMANITARIAN: FOR ANYONE WHO IS SUFFERING NO ERA HAS BEEN WORSE

///

"not now" Tina Modotti
told Manuel Álvarez Bravo after
he tried to give her a camera and darkroom
        it was cavalier to get off the moving train but my wrists
protected my hips as we all hit a newly tilled garden   ya maybe you can't
        go home again   or step in the same river twice
the rapidity of accrued cells formed a river monster

of grief

YOU CAN'T BOARD AGAIN
LOOKING LIKE THIS

in a deft move against collective insanity I scrubbed glochids from her shoulder
       some of which lodged in my fingertips   a truer love pact not involving blood
but soap
and water

///

          people quit
               people quit and people start

          the root of Americanism
            Amnesia

///

ELDER WOMAN AT THE POST OFFICE: YOU GET A DIME BACK
ME: WHAT WILL I DO?
ELDER WOMAN: REBUILD AND COME BACK AND SEE ME

power hates when it realizes it is being moved slowly to do certain things
       that disrupt accumulation
we pray certain entities never know we exist
       even if it feels like we'll perish (publish or...)

responsibility is the ability to respond (Duncan)
     which requires the space for unpredictable gestures
to the elite city
     I was no devotee
though I took notes
     like one

                            ///

         rapture in   a leak   line drying   a sour
              rag on the fan   cobwebs that indicate vacated
        spiders   catching and releasing
             a young lizard   wearing black in   the sun   (the Bedouin
        would know)   sweeping dust with a straw broom   and oh the novelty
             of an outdoor hose to clean the stoop   of the four-plex
        where we are the only tenants   vacancy so gently
             troubling to a New York nervous
        system   trading "real estate hell"
             for a place becoming
        too hot to live

     ///

"begin where I must
     from the failure of systems"

the hundreds of tales I know

are no good to anybody
        anymore

        PAMPINEA: AND IF WE RETURN TO OUR HOMES WHAT HAPPENS?

why would his mother discard his archive
        on a West Village corner
why is there often an angel who walks past and locks energies with it
        or one who breaks in the front door
but days too late

///

        some European shepherds used stilts to better observe their flocks
from a distance hence shepherd spiders have long legs but what we have here
        is a solitary cellar spider who has built a ropey web
from the pipes to a wide brimmed hat

        today P. said "some people need their nominations desperately"
my love adds "we smell fusty to them" as if cosmic time has nothing to do with current events
        my insider friend revealed that she can speedread upside down
how much they make and how much they pay   capitalism's scribes   over time makes you
        kinda awful

I have never seen her move but I see her work
        some spiders bob to shake their webs when threatened   and then there is autonomy
when they release a leg that has been grasped by an external agent

///

days held by sartorial routine
      mesh bag of used smocks
pushing the limits of doing the opposite of what we're supposed to do
      to be useless in building your earned income
and have a right to shelter   I noticed neon letters from a small window
      while taking a shower   OLIV— the arm of a crane a block away
going slower
      seeing only the one I love
and slower
      only errands
the house is porous
      (best home I ever had
person viewing upstairs unit: "it's falling apart")
      animals find their way in and out
I walk around the dirt lot with my shirt undone
      like this is woman's land

///

      to read for pleasure not scouting or anything
        to read the books my friends write free of anything

///

perhaps the monkeys would cut us some slack
      while the rats would argue to consign us to hell
to settle the political score   to take a neutral smell
      like cherry blossom and traumatize a being to that smell
to watch it fuck up three generations   robbed of our animal sense
      of NOW   made a cusp of tension
         is not exactly
       living   DEMOCRACY
                   A JOY THAT HURTS

///

"The old ones did not believe that the passage of years caused old age."
      Leslie Marmon Silko wrote on the first page of "Tucson
Book One" in *Almanac of the Dead*

      "possessed by a nameless acceleration"
Etel Adnan wrote in "Baalbeck" in *Time*

      dream : when the lavender-eyed hawk soared
she saw who was still around
     all records auto-expunged
in the people vs. witches
     my this-and-that authority torn
digested and redistributed
     hair the color of wood

or a brindle coat
a face hard to place
in the scheme

///

serial dream : fastidiously sewing garments for poets
creating a look that anticipates a viable avant-garde
I was cured of imposter syndrome
when I realized no one wanted to wear what I wore
a blank cape that would only read as scrumptious
a woman made of herbed meat and potatoes
rising from petty moments is a ritual
well-wishes to young souls in their crowns

///

alliteration makes authoritarianism too cute
"dastardly deeds"
infects even my dishwashing
the truest depiction of a politician
Phil Hartman playing Reagan playing Reagan
who cares what's real anymore
"voice is mostly murder"   genius is whatever
are heartbreak and gravitas synonymous
is boredom the poultice
can I spy on my self-exile

the brown mouse I just saw
                had 8 and a half x 11 flames in her eyes

///

who knows what any person does withdrawn
            if a city can exist only because it is beautiful so can
this state of mind   witnessed by wilderness
            no mind payed to inherent paradox
naming myself eremite blasphemer
            Transcend and Organize!
I'm out on the street
            as poet, ah [sob]
            and as citizen [another sob]
organize or be organized
            in hell
by the incoherent
            shadow admin
shadow friend

///

POET: ADDRESS THE UNSPEAKABLE

what Dante saw and did wandering Italy
            in Florentine exile   fleshed out Beatrice's
you are not on the earth as you believe

transcendence converts us to foolhardy
lovers plowing connotative byways
        our words shooting "amiable love arrows"
at every thing

        what Pasolini saw and did as a Roman
driven out of Friuli   ambiguous scripture of the living still
        life   the   long take   imagine moments reproducing
simultaneously from various viewpoints
        to solve his own murder

what power-crazed rulers saw and did
        as power-crazed rulers
with no option of the wise
        but as power-crazed rulers
just power-crazed rulers

                ///

        no one tells you how anticlimactic it is to achieve
your goals   it would be anti-American   the people's will moves toward transient
        amnesia   who doesn't love to invent the wheel?
when I was a toddler raw force supplanting law was televised
        a lawyer and a politician scuffled over the words "actual" and "literal"
to talk about a crime   can something actually happen but not literally?
        they cultivate their own historians
and poets   I don't have the credentials to be either
        but now I can refuse to have dinner with whomever I want

///

a rock that looks like a gumball reminds me that I am being protected
        by who I don't know   my love left with blue laced agate in her bra today
the first of October has passed and we are still the only residents
        in this atypical abode   homebodies   with prosperity candles aflame
I peered through the drape of my work room each time I heard
        car wheels on a gravel road

///

it's a concept that the people you imagine   are in an office space together
        people in office space together are radical
doing stand-up and speaking in a spontaneous prose style
        community is experimental
it's a disadvantage not to have one if you're experimental
        where I will barter you a blog post for a book
and an advantage not to have one if you're guarding the story
        that you sprang from Zeus's head

///

IF YOU HAVE THE CAPACITY TO RESIST
BEING DUMBED DOWN
NOW IS THE TIME TO OPTIMIZE IT

i.e. pop out your abnormal eye

///

option of the wise   to write your comedy

when every star vanishes from the eastern
        sky excepting Lucifer (Greek: Phosphorus)

record keeping allowed me to not look back
        when I didn't have designated and carnal punishers

(distinct from God   or   the government…) carnal and humdrum
        humdrum and quotidian   then   I agreed to epic self-

harm   in the elite city   kitchen is the first to go
        the tinnitus is memory of clanging pots and pans
who just wants to be adored?

        Demons   Poets

///

MAN AT FARMERS MARKET: WE ACCEPT WOOD TOKENS AS MONEY
AND WE GIVE SAWDUST FOR CHANGE

ELDER WOMAN AT POST OFFICE: $19.05   SOUNDS LIKE A BAD YEAR

///

...so in 1966 he opened the church to the wandering poets...
believing they were doing real theology
      amidst an onslaught of do-gooders
"The system that works is
      one of the forgotten"
in delirium grandma wants her teaching job back
      my Poles yearn for their work
it's forgotten because of who
      it works for
politics determined by how narrow you read
      am I eligible?   or not

do homework against the grain
do homework against the grain
you know what I mean

      my account will run dry before
she who is one-hundred

///

      I went to an event and saw people who resembled
        people I used to know
      I also resembled myself the way age
        and weight can make us unrecognizable
      but none of them knew me then   or now

                                   the woman who looks like a poet
                         I admired finds a chair
                         I find a chair

            ///

I escape the bind of good and evil
        when *there are nights that don't ever happen*
knee deep in
                gems
                ferns
                reptilian life

    well-being in an egg
I don't carry the fantasy of the unbearable you

                ultraviolet
                light

                                                    ///

                here we are   specious connections of the politician
                        issued at the rate of 13 per day
                seeping into the language arts
                        say homelessness causes water pollution
                a wall is beautiful
                        or a womb can move freely
                an animal inside an animal

///

where you come from and who you are needs to be
        aggressively devalued for poetry to be a thing
for poetry to be a thing poetry ceases to be about innovation
        for a THING can be funded
can be made into a shape that history can be made into
        can be made into a program
that conspires to limit the spaces of livelihood
        but we have found them living
on the edges of state universities
        reading between the lines
I haven't been hazed so how can I haze anyone?

///

        the gorgeous group of iguanas were under the console
                in a nest of sandals and sawdust guarding one egg
        there were hornworms nearby
                but iguanas are herbivores so maybe these were giant
        geckos? the egg looked like blown glass or an Easter egg
                the night before I had stunned a water bug in our medicine
        cabinet with the binding of a book by Vestrini and sent it down the drain
                in the dream I was just as vigilant to the nest
        as they were   making those worms appear
                making sure a dog I no longer have
        kept his distance

///

R. sent me a photo of a painting that she saw in a museum in Angers
      "The Listener" by Alexis Mérodack-Jeanneau   she said he was like us
and I know she means that it has often been detrimental
      to be devoted to promoting the work of others
you'll be known as a poet's poet
      which I will here define as a poet
who isn't interested in the style of hunger
      that is base
and insatiable

///

A MURDER OF CROWS

A GAGGLE OF GEESE

A CREW OF HUSTLERS

///

how to lay low
      in day-glow   in blood-boil
I don't want to
      be pained   so I think hey

I'm like a punk

who made a splash
I'm a punk
who was a flash
I'm a punk
I have a pan

/ / /

each energumen has a soft-spoken enabler
they care more about "you" than for you
(you, the person you) the thing you
occupying a sociological space where your
art never resolves the problems of your personhood
the regime is friendly
to your art

/ / /

if you didn't think cacti were beings before…

sick allegorical minds   plow down
a girl scaled   a replica   of the wall
"in about a minute"

///

the sound was displaced in my adulthood
        boys playing football
I listened aggressively   painfully close   a trigger for cinematic flashback
        to a time when I drew plays on the palm of my hand
staving off everything I had to become
        in city
        after city
        after
        city
after having left the most elite of them
        I better understood my nature

///

my poems take up more and more page
        the size of the book makes it awkward to stock
old age is a fait accompli
        all of my measurements expand

TAILOR: THAT'S A LOT OF MATERIAL

an astrologist said an asteroid in my birth sky means
        come spring 2020 any problems I've had
around community and self-worth will feel like
        an IMAX experience

to edit the weird (you too are weird) is to waste the past
     165 years

it smelled different in the back of the house this morning
     down saturated with dark roast and creosote

maybe you think everything is fine

///

     messengers shove primo poetry propaganda into the boxes of MFAs
she says she'll have their attention for 10 weeks but how can we compete
     with hypnotics
to keep poetry serving the nation by being a parody
     of poetry serving a parody of leadership
a poet's shoddy lament *the poets are dying*   spread widely by the elite
     city's coveted rag

POETS NEVER DIE
     my friends

///

the train runs on a schedule less transparent than church bells
      audible from any point I've rested my head in this town
my body clock unwittingly geared to it
      in honor of she who took me to a ranch behind the waffle house
and reset me
      I left my orange peels in a line and we   looking like a fabled couple
counted backward
      I too have said things other than what I meant
adding to the farcical proceedings of the collect

///

      the terror of the poet was certain
         palpable in equal
to zero dollars
         and may have moved
zero hearts
         what is amazing
express your desire
         to be forgotten
as a person
         yet still do your 24/7
listen to the music
         of centuries rising
above the mushroom time

///

a mouse gnawing at the back of the stove woke me
        you think this is the way it is now
MOUSE: THIS TOO SHALL PASS
        I saw the half acre dirt yard as a perfect
site for a series   so set up a camera and tried to capture
        myself the way I am
the way I was and the way I want to be
        recognized   a slightly misaligned being
releasing soul   new pink sodium-vapor bulbs under dark sky ordinance
        strings of lights on cacti unrelated to holiday
in a socially impossible milieu   I threw style to the hot wind
        I saw the astronomy with my naked eye

///

November

        the fire in Paradise
super typhoon Yolanda

GERMAN ACTIVISTS SEND TRUMP A PIECE OF BERLIN WALL

///

petrified   by petrified
        wood   and pomegranate

the entire apartment turned into a mantel

        the new tenants upstairs flood us with energy
we guess they used to live in a house

        the height of my true self
knows when to grow and when to shrink
        and when you have to do both at the same time
till it's no strain at all
        it's   *fluid as past saviors*
        poetry

all of my tics recorded for posterity

///

                    where are places on the edge of disaster and high taxes
                            that have X Y and Z?   what to do with all this
                    wool? I have played with fat and perhaps this time
                            in mid-journey   lost
                    where are places beyond the purview of "god-
                            led" leaders   lest we be smart as octopi
                    making daring escape

///

it can take 700 years to WHEN PIGS FLY IN THE AYRE WITH THEIR TAYLES FORWARD
       to be pardoned
your murder may be solved
       WHEN PIGS FLY IN THE AYRE WITH THEIR TAYLES FORWARD
and it won't even be called a cold case
       thugs convene daily in public parks
loaded with technology of the era
       let's weaponize _____!
i.e. infuse everything with the sweet smell
       of death-drive
it can be a rosebush
       a kiosk
it can be a nonprofit invisibly steering
       your movement

///

       early morning half-dream :
              I blew the dust (skulls) off of a book of desirable poems
       in a box of desirable books
           somewhere else a book
       is waiting   I drove through the red dust
           without knowing the time
       past a group of women who marched toward the same sundown
          oh   it's eternity
       the problem eternally being
          laws
               on my body

///

make space with buoyance
      you and your lover will always be swept into what people think
upthrust your word choice
      what they think you think based on their mishandling
hold the space for your lover   a babe in a lake   three bodies of water
      part of the sky   (you are not Chicken Little)
you and your lover masquerade as mild people
      and no one ever asks you what you think
friends nor
creep-a-zoids

///

dream : a scene appeared on my forearm in the form of a sleeve
      the ink asking for my visual intelligence
a green leafy limb   fueled by desire in the trunk
      today I may qualify for Medicaid unable to predict
income for 2020   I talked to four people at one store
      about the whereabouts of an electric kettle

///

it's a seller's market (suburban)
      ancient aquifers are dropping
the diurnal freight train puts me in a less personal mood

than the nocturnal train
but it's all conveyance (commerce)
sped up to tear up
human bodies   hex the owners
shriek one time
the words become something horned
outside barricade

(Sean Bonney in memoriam)

/ / /

our details don't matter
    that's what they take
clearly I do things that are wrong
    a story is what I will never give anyone
nonlinearity is my protection
    a line of automated fire
wrong place wrong time
don't lady me

/ / /

November got noisy with people
    the colder days
the dimmer light
    the citrus is ripe
two quarters of a squeezed lime

    lay in the dirt
an endless Sunday night
        party
men in white trucks (or that is the
        form in which they appear to me) speed
down the partition
        as we spin (further) from the light

                                        ///

                        I'm going to live my life this way
                                language arrives   attention to commonplace
                        can that energy age us
                                differently?   keep old souls youthful?
                        you can look at yourself
                                more closely from a distance
                        having left documents
                                to let go of former selves   and their demands
                        still all I want
                                is for my friends   to read me

        ///

gave me a start   thinking it was another
        mouse   it was
a dust bunny   A. ended another letter
        "where are you?"   busy
being a body   oh that's…   what are you

doing?   I'm busy being a body *here*
busy as a dust bunny play-bowing
        to things animated by wind

NOTES ON POEMS

My poems are usually loaded with references to other poems and I haven't always thought it important to point them out. During the writing of this book, however, the work of favored writers, living and dead, brought me especially deep companionship. With gratitude, I name as many as I can trace, and offer the names to you for further reading and listening.

"FUN METER" – "broke the bed fucking" and "die fucking…" are both Alice Notley's from the poem "April" and a notebook of hers in the UCSD archive, respectively. Thank you to Cassandra Gillig for sharing this archival gold with me. "Upper limit fucking" is a riff on Zukofsky's "upper limit music" in "A-12." "Green leaves over a heart in ruins…" and "Spira, spera" are from Victor Hugo's *The Hunchback of Notre Dame*. "My crow Pluto" is a reference to Marianne Moore's poem "To Victor Hugo of My Crow Pluto." "Stirred for birds" and lines that follow riff on Gerard Manley Hopkins in "The Windhover." "We have always known you wanted us" is from H.D.'s "The Helmsman." "Airy devilship" is from Henry Purcell's "She Loves and She Confesses." "Who gave me the note?" is from Robert Duncan's "The Windings" and "You will often tell the story…" is from his "The Architecture Passages 9."

"CENTURION FACE" – "One more poem if you think you can handle it" is a comment Alice Notley made before reading "At Night the States" in Buffalo, 1987, archived on PennSound. The last line of this poem merges Allen Ginsberg's description of The Poetry Project and a line from his poem "Howl."

"GRANZINO THE SECOND" – "B: Am I being clear?..." is banter between Bernadette Mayer, the featured poet, and Anne Waldman, who was in the audience. The recording is archived on PennSound but I can't recall which one. "Mid hriff" is Robert Duncan's spelling of "midriff" in "The Torso Passages 18." "But you shall not escape my iambics" is from Catullus. Granzino was the name of Frida Kahlo's pet deer.

"BLOOD OF A POET" – "Lesbian mode" is from "Barbara Hammer's Exit Interview" in *The New Yorker*. "I know the names…" is from Pasolini's "I Know" published in the Italian newspaper *Il Corrierre Della Sera* and translated by Giovanni Tiso at overland.org.au. "The World is of infinitely great roughness" is a quotation by Benoit Mandelbrot. "Whatever can come to a woman can come to me" is from Muriel Rukeyser's "Waterlily Fire." "A walking grove of trees" is from Phillip Whalen's "Since You Ask Me."

"STOP MAKING PEACE" – "Enter freely, Go safely…" is from Bram Stoker's *Dracula*.

"ANTIPOETRY" – "The whole thing began…" is from Nicanor Parra's "The Last Battle" as is the concept of Antipoetry.

"FAMOUS HERMITS" – "Begin where I must…" is from Robert Duncan's "After a Long Illness." The line from Pampinea is from Boccaccio's *Decameron*. "Voice is mostly murder" is from Heriberto Yepez's "On Imperial Poetics: Baraka's Defense of Olson." "Amiable love arrows" is from Lyn Hejinian's "The Rejection of Closure." "I'm out on the street…" is from Pasolini's "A Desperate Vitality." "The system that works…" and "do homework against the grain" are from John Godfrey's "The System" and a personal email from the poet, respectively. "There are nights…" is from Alda Merini's "Aphorisms." "They care more about you…" is from Prageeta Sharma's "Poetry Anonymous." "Listen to the music…" is from Bob Kaufman's "Believe, Believe." "Fluid as past saviors" is from Cedar Sigo's "Three Portraits." "As we spin…" is from Diane di Prima's "Revolutionary Letter #57."

ACKNOWLEDGEMENTS

I started writing this book in January 2018 in Missoula, MT while I was a visiting writer at the University of Montana, on the territories of the Salish and Kalispel people, and finished it in November 2019 in Tucson, AZ, traditional homelands of the Tohono O'odham Nation and lands of the Pascua Yaqui Tribe.

Some of these poems have been published in *Bæst: a journal of queer forms & affects*, *Blazing Stadium*, *The Canary*, *Harp & Altar*, *Hyperallergic*, *mid hriff*, *A Perfect Vacuum*, Futurepoem's blog *futurefeed*, as part of Woodland Pattern Book Center's project "Prompts Against Anxiety," and *The Tiny*. I'm grateful for the opportunities I've had during the coronavirus pandemic to share sections of this work virtually: Brooklyn Rail's New Social Environment series and their Radical Poetry Readings series, Center for Contemporary Art Santa Fe, and the Marble Hill Camera Club.

Thank you to the Foundation for Contemporary Arts for supporting my work with a Grants to Artists Award in 2019, and to Prageeta Sharma and Rachel Levitsky for being poetic inspirations. Thank you also to Kyle Dacuyan for sending me a recording of Agnes Martin's talk at The Poetry Project that I didn't know existed.

This book is for, in the deepest sense, Kimberly Alidio.

MORE FROM ARCHWAY EDITIONS

Ishmael Reed – *The Haunting of Lin-Manuel Miranda*
Unpublishable (edited by Chris Molnar and Etan Nechin)
Gabriel Kruis – *Acid Virga*
Erin Taylor – *Bimboland*
NDA: An Autofiction Anthology (edited by Caitlin Forst)
Mike Sacks – *Randy*
Mike Sacks – *Stinker Lets Loose*
Paul Schrader – *First Reformed*
Archways 1 (edited by Chris Molnar and Nicodemus Nicoludis)
Brantly Martin – *Highway B: Horrorfest*
cokemachineglow (edited by Clayton Purdom)
Ishmael Reed – *Life Among the Aryans*
Alice Notley – *Runes and Chords*

Archway Editions can be found at your local bookstore or ordered directly through Simon & Schuster.

Questions? Comments? Concerns? Send correspondence to:

Archway Editions
c/o powerHouse Books
220 36th St., Building #2
Brooklyn, NY
11232